Why Am I Dancing Alone?

— by —
Sue Kovach

Contents

Why Am I Dancing Alone? 7

Curing Your Loneliness 11

Raise Your Self-Esteem 28

Feel Comfortable By Yourself 48

How To Attract Someone Special
  Into Your Life 69

How To Keep Someone
  In Your Life 90

Why Am I Dancing Alone?

Does it seem everyone else in the world has a partner? Do you see couples having intimate dinners in restaurants, dancing the night away at nightclubs, bike riding through the park, strolling through shopping malls? Everywhere you look, do you see couples having fun and living full, happy lives together? Do you feel left out? Do you wonder where your partner is – why you're dancing alone?

What's most troubling is that you can't figure out why you're alone. You ask yourself the same questions over and over: What's wrong with me? Why doesn't anyone want me? Why don't other people have these problems? Is there anyone out there for me? Did I do something wrong? How can I change things? Will I be alone forever?

Let's look at what we mean by "alone." In this case, we're talking about not being part of a loving, romantic relationship. You want to be part of a couple and that's perfectly normal. Everyone wants to feel loved, needed and wanted in that way. And if you feel that a relationship is what's lacking in your life, you're feeling the pangs of loneliness.

Do any of these sentences describe you?

❇ I don't feel like going out to places where there are lots of couples having fun.

❇ I watch lots of television and movies and fantasize about relationships with the actors I see.

❇ I daydream about having a relationship with my "ideal" man.

❇ I feel envious of my friends who have husbands or lovers.

❇ I used to wear makeup, but don't usually bother anymore.

❇ My favorite clothes to wear most of the time are my worn-out sweats (or cut-off jeans and a T-shirt).

❇ Sometimes, I don't like myself very much.

❇ I think I'm doing something wrong because no one wants me.

❇ I feel depressed, rundown, bored, fatigued or empty inside.

❇ Sometimes I feel scared and anxious.

❇ I cry easily.

If you relate to some or any of these sentences, you may be down in the dumps and feeling blue because you're lonely. You may feel despair now, but the good news is that you can come out of the dumps and banish your loneliness! You can even feel more comfortable being alone and this is good because getting more comfortable with yourself in all situations is one of the first steps toward bringing a real, loving relationship into your life.

You need to know that feeling loneliness and being alone are two different things! You can be lonely in a crowd of people and you can also be alone and feel wonderful about yourself and your life. If you're reading this book, what you're suffering from is loneliness.

You'll learn that you don't have to dance through life alone, and you can start on the road to your new life right now.

What's wrong with me?

Why doesn't anyone want me?

Did I do something wrong?

Why don't other people have these problems?

You're feeling so alone and these questions keep coming up in your mind. Of course it's easy to think that there's something wrong with you, that you're somehow out of step with the rest of the world. And this is part of your problem.

"In our society, loneliness is a secret we keep – sometimes from ourselves," says Dr. Anne Peplau, Ph.D., a professor of social psychology at UCLA who has studied the subject for 20 years. In an April 1991 article in *Ladies Home Journal,* Dr. Peplau discusses loneliness and how people perceive those who are lonely.

"Loneliness has a stigma attached to it," she says. "There's an assumption out there that if you're lonely, it must be your own fault. Otherwise, you'd certainly have lots of friends, right?"

Dr. Peplau says that loneliness is triggered when our need for a close, caring relationship isn't fulfilled.

"At any given time, at least 10 percent of the population feels lonely," she says.

So, it's good to know that, ironically, you're not alone in your loneliness! The wonderful reality is that there's nothing wrong with you and you didn't do anything wrong. You're no different from millions of other people who find themselves without a relationship and, after a while, realize that they're lonely. Other people do have the same relationship doubts, anxieties and worries that you're having.

But that doesn't change the fact that you're down in the dumps and not feeling very good about yourself. And this is another part of your problem.

Can you cure your loneliness and bring someone wonderful into your life? Yes! If you no longer want to dance alone, here are the steps you need to take:

1. "Cure" your feelings of loneliness.
2. Feel better about yourself and raise your self-esteem and self-confidence.
3. Feel comfortable being by yourself. (Yes, in order to not be alone, you must enjoy being alone!)
4. Attract someone into your life.
5. Keep that special someone in your life.

Anyone who feels lonely can overcome the feelings in a simple way: by focusing on growing from your experience rather than focusing on your feelings. In this book, you'll learn a lot of ways to grow from your experiences and read about how others grew from theirs. You'll learn that you're not alone in your loneliness and that you can find someone to dance with for a very long time to come.

Curing Your Loneliness

You're feeling a lot of pain from loneliness. It's difficult to get motivated toward making any changes in your life because you're feeling so down and blue. Well, you're going to learn how to pull yourself out of the doldrums and banish loneliness from your life so you can get started on finding your perfect dance partner!

Let's Talk About Loneliness

Maxine, a 44-year-old real estate agent, describes how loneliness feels to her:

"The worst time is at night. I'm a nocturnal sort of person and I can make my own hours for work, so I like to stay up late and sleep late. Late at night, when everyone else in my apartment complex has gone to bed and everything is so still and quiet – *that's* when it hits me. I feel like I'm the last person on earth. I think about my day and realize there's no one else in my life. I look forward to my night alone in my bed and wonder why this is happening to me, why my life didn't quite work out the way I thought it would.

"I thought I'd be married, have children. I don't even have a relationship with a man who's a good friend, let alone a friend and lover. And the older I get, the more painful it is to be without that, to be alone.

"Sometimes when I think about it, my very bones ache. It hurts to swallow because I have a lump in my throat. I don't know if there's anything I can do to take away this pain."

Twenty-eight-year-old Jackie, a secretary at an engineering firm, describes her loneliness this way:

"It's almost like that gnawing at your stomach you get when you're really hungry, except this has nothing to do with hunger pangs. These are pangs of loneliness. If I'm lying in bed with the lights out, trying to fall asleep and I get that feeling, I curl up and hug my knees. It's like I'm trying to protect myself. And for all the gnawing inside, I often wonder what can possibly be gnawed at because I feel so empty inside, too. Like there's nothing there. I don't know if anything can ever fill it up."

Darlene, a 42-year-old schoolteacher, wrote this in her journal:

"Sometimes I get scared – really, really scared. I can be lying in bed, lights on and suddenly I'm aware that I'm scared and I can feel the panic start to creep in. And the amazing thing is that I have absolutely no idea what I'm scared of.

"Maybe I become aware of my aloneness and that scares me. Maybe I'm afraid that I'll always be alone, that no one will ever want me. I become acutely aware of the fact that at this time, at this point in my life, I've never had anyone who really cared. Why should I think that suddenly someone will appear when, up until now, he never has? I wish I had somewhere to go to hide from the pain."

These women are experiencing real pain – the pain of loneliness. They miss having a relationship in their lives, yet both sound as if they believe they're powerless to do anything about it. Their pain seems to be stronger than any desires they may have to take action and make changes in their lives – and they don't think there could be anything worse.

Right now, you probably don't want to be told that there are worse things than being alone. You don't even believe that. What could possibly be worse than this pain and heartache? Than this longing to share your life with someone, to touch and to hold someone? Well, there really are plenty of things that are worse, things over which you have no control.

Believe it or not, you *do* have control over your loneliness. You can take control and change the emptiness in your life by taking some simple, positive steps.

But you've tried that before, haven't you? You've done things you thought would comfort you and discovered you actually make yourself feel worse! Your happily married friends invite you to go out with them – you love your friends and certainly accept their invitation. But when you see the two of them together and how happy they are, it makes you feel bad about yourself and your own situation! Your feelings of loneliness became more intense and painful.

Even spending holidays with your family has the opposite effect that you thought it would. Holidays can be stressful times and getting together with family can actually emphasize to you that you don't have a relationship in your life. Once again, something you thought could make you feel better, make you feel happy, backfires on you.

Don't despair. Everyone suffers from loneliness and

everyone goes through times when they have no relationship. So there's nothing wrong with you.

In order to understand your own feelings, let's first look at what loneliness really means.

More women suffer from loneliness than men. Berkeley, California psychotherapist Emily Hancock, author of *The Girl Within,* a study of women's identity, said in an article in the February 1994 *Cosmopolitan* magazine: "In my practice, I see women going to great lengths to make sure they don't have time alone. They'll call up five or 10 people – people they're not even friends with – just so they won't have to face an afternoon or evening by themselves."

Paulette S. And Her Superficial Friends

Paulette S. is a perfect example of someone who couldn't face being alone. An extremely busy independent television producer, Paulette, 31, was rarely seen alone. She had a large contingent of friends and a collection of boyfriends. This impressed Sarah, a 38-year-old writer who had made Paulette's acquaintance through a colleague. Sarah and Paulette became good friends, but as the two women grew closer, Sarah began to realize something: She rarely saw Paulette's other friends except on weekends at trendy nightclubs, when everyone tended to gather together as a group.

Sarah also noticed that sometimes Paulette was more of a presence in her life than others. It took a while for Sarah to understand what was going on, but once she did, she was very surprised.

"I'd always thought Paulette was incredibly popular because she seemed to have so many friends around her," says Sarah. "What I was amazed to learn was that almost none of these people was really a 'friend' to Paulette. They were casual acquaintances at best. In fact, some of the people that Paulette talked about the most turned out to be people whose last names she didn't even know!"

Sarah, on the other hand, had only two or three really close friends. But they were people she'd been close with for many years, as far back as her high school and college days.

"I'm perfectly comfortable with my few close, but long-time friends rather than having a slew of superficial acquaintances like Paulette had," Sarah says. "But Paulette, it turns out, is so afraid of being alone, she'd rather have someone – anyone – around her to keep from being lonely. What she didn't realize is that by having all these superficial relationships, including superficial love relationships, she was lonelier than she'd have probably been without the whole lot of them!"

This is why Paulette clung to Sarah, her only true close friend. It was the only thing that relieved some of her loneliness. And sometimes Paulette clung way too much!

Once, Sarah was abruptly awakened at 2:00 a.m. by a loud pounding on her front door. She went to the door to find Paulette, who tearfully told her she'd broken up with her latest boyfriend. Sarah quickly ushered Paulette inside, made her a cup of tea and sat down to listen to her story, thinking she'd be up half the night. It took Paulette only five minutes to tell everything she had to say!

"This 'boyfriend' was one of Paulette's superficial relationships. Yet she was so distraught by them breaking up that she was compelled to come to my house, no matter what time it was!" Sarah recalls. "At this point, I realized it was the perfect opportunity to try to tell Paulette what her life and relationships looked like through my eyes."

The two women did indeed talk through most of the night and Paulette spent the rest of the night in Sarah's guest room. The next day, she admitted to Sarah that she needed to rethink many of her relationships and begin to acknowledge that she had problems with being alone. Sarah felt she'd finally made a breakthrough with her friend, whom she really did care about.

It's obvious that Paulette would do anything to keep from being alone. Her busy life, however, kept her from making true connections with people, especially men. So no matter how many people she surrounded herself with, she felt alone.

In the April 1991 issue of *Ladies Home Journal*, Evelyn Moschetta, D.S.W., a New York-based psychotherapist, said: "There's a big difference between being busy and being connected. Many women today are very, very busy, but they don't have enough truly genuine relationships, people with whom they can be totally open, who accept and love them for who they really are. That's the basis of real friendship. And it's missing today in a fundamental way."

A Friends Network – A Cure For Loneliness

Bette Midler, "The Divine Miss M," sang a wonderful, uplifting song entitled *You've Got To Have Friends*. This is absolutely true! So how can Paulette – and you

– make real friendship connections and cure the loneliness? By developing a social network that includes a few close friends or at least two or three close confidants, that's how.

Says Paulette: "I knew I had to reach out to people and really make a connection, but in order to do that, I had to let them really get to know me. That was difficult at first because I'd been hurt so many times, I didn't want to open myself up to being hurt again.

"This was especially true with men. I simply couldn't connect, so I made 'surface' relationships with virtually every man I met. But no one could understand the loneliness I felt deep down inside. Only Sarah, my one true friend, knew what I was doing and cared.

"So I took some great advice and while I don't have nearly as many people around me as I used to, the friends I do have are 'real' friends. Just like Sarah. And you know what? I'm finally getting to know a really great man. He's the only one in my life right now – isn't that a change? – but he's definitely going to be worth it. I'm slowing down and taking my time."

Paulette got on the right track. Here's how to develop and maintain a network of friends, using some of the tips Paulette followed and some others from Dr. John DeFrain, a clinical family psychologist and researcher:

1. Don't stay locked in your house – get out and meet people. Go to places where networks of people with common interests are already formed, such as professional societies, clubs and support groups. These organizations have social functions you can attend, which generally have a lighter, social atmosphere that helps friendships evolve naturally.

2. Make friends with people anywhere you go, whether you travel for business or take a vacation. Even if someone lives on the other side of the country, says DeFrain, it doesn't mean that person can't help you personally. "Distance is not a factor when you're looking for good friends," he said.

3. Cultivate your new friendships by being a good friend yourself. Friendship is a give-and-take situation and you can't just expect your friends to be there for you. You must reciprocate. "You can't be draining energy from your friends all the time," advised DeFrain. "You have to reach out and be a friend, too. Work on your friendship skills. For any relationship to last for very long, it has to be reciprocal."

4. Learn to be a good listener because listening to others shows genuine concern for them. How many times has your loneliness manifested itself with you needing desperately to talk to someone who would simply listen? Said DeFrain: "We all need someone to bounce our personal and professional problems off of. If you're willing to be a good listener, others will be good listeners for you when you need them."

5. Don't keep an account of what you and your friends have done for each other. This is one sure way to defeat a give-and-take friendship, said DeFrain. "Things balance out in the long run. Don't be afraid to ask your friends for help, but be willing to reciprocate when they need you. Friendship has to be a two-way street."

6. Take time to know your friends well enough to be sensitive to their moods and problems. This makes you someone your friends are comfortable to be with – and be totally themselves with, DeFrain said. "To really get to know somebody, put yourself in their place," he suggested. "Feel how their life feels and then you know them. That takes sensitivity and effort, but if you start to do it on a regular basis, it's wonderful! You find so many different, good things by trying to understand the world from somebody else's perspective."

7. Make more time for your friends. Set aside time during the day if you can or after work to make a phone call to at least one friend, at least once a day. Connections stay strong when they're reinforced. Schedule it in on your daily calendar that you must make a phone call at a certain time. And be sure to get together with your friend (or friends) at least once or twice a week, if possible.

Is There More Than One Kind Of Loneliness?

There are actually two types of loneliness, according to Robert S. Weiss, Ph.D., a research professor at the University of Massachusetts in Boston and a pioneer in loneliness research. In an article in the April 1991 *Ladies Home Journal,* Dr. Weiss says loneliness can be both emotional and social.

Social loneliness is when we simply don't want to be alone, but would rather be with other people. This can be family, friends, lovers, colleagues – anyone.

Emotional loneliness happens when we aren't sharing our life with someone else, a person Dr. Weiss calls an attachment figure. This can be a husband or lover. Weiss says this type of loneliness can even cause physical symptoms, such as restlessness or heaviness in the chest.

In an article in *SOLO Lifestyles for Singles,* a web magazine for single people (www.solosingles.com), Pat McChristie writes that emotional loneliness is usually the hardest to cure, for the following reasons:

1. People are afraid of rejection and therefore are scared of developing close relationships. All close relationships require you to be open about yourself and that leaves you open to being hurt.

2. Love relationships – or any close relationship – needs a "spark," or chemistry, the feeling you get when you meet someone that says the two of you have "clicked." It becomes a numbers game, writes McChristie.

"We need to meet a lot of people to find our kindred spirits. Meeting a lot of people requires a lot of effort. And it does not happen quickly."

3. People are generally competitive and having close relationships requires you to not be competitive. This can be difficult for many people.

Maxine, the real estate agent I wrote about earlier, felt the physical symptoms of emotional loneliness. She described her loneliness as "an ache in my very bones." She really did feel this pain, but had no idea where it came from. Maxine visited her doctor several times and each time he could find nothing wrong except for noticing that Maxine was feeling low. He asked her about stress and anxiety in her life, suggesting it might be causing her physical pains.

"I brushed him off with a short laugh," Maxine says.

"I didn't think I had any problems in my life. I was happy with my job, my home life, everything – or so I was kidding myself! The truth is, each time one of my two close friends went out with her boyfriend, I felt resentful. Even angry!"

Maxine was about to call a specialist about her pains, when she saw an article in a magazine that gave her pause to think. The title was: "I'm So Lonely, It Hurts." She read the article and realized she'd been fooling herself about her life.

"I knew I had to pull myself up by my bootstraps and make some changes," she recalls. "I knew I had to do something. The more I sat around feeling sorry for myself, letting myself sink further and further into depression, the harder I knew it would be to bring a man into my life. Who would want to be close to such a lonely, depressed wreck?"

The first thing Maxine did was call all of her friends to catch up on the phone. She hadn't done that for a while and she realized she had a lot of catching up to do. Next, she made dates to see each and every one of them.

Why did she do this? Because she'd stopped making connections – real connections.

Some Quick Cures To Get You Going

Are you afraid of being alone? Do you feel uncomfortable or anxious if you're home alone at night or on weekends? Do you go to the mall or any store and walk aimlessly amongst people to avoid being alone? If so, there are some "quick cures" you can do to take the edge off. Here, according to SOLO Singles online magazine (www.solosingles.com) are some common quick cures for loneliness:

- 🌹 Get a pet. But make sure you can truly commit to caring for a pet.

- 🌹 Call your friends, old and new, nearby or far away. Engage in long conversations, even superficial ones at this point, to pass some time.

- 🌹 Take up some new hobbies. Do something you've always wanted to do, like take an art class or learn to play a musical instrument.

- 🌹 Pamper yourself with a trip to a spa or go on a shopping trip. But be careful – don't over-shop just because you're feeling low!

- 🌹 Check out your local singles' scene. This includes churches that sponsor singles' parties, local organizations with regular gatherings for singles, sports clubs specifically for singles. You can immediately meet other people who are going through the same feelings of loneliness as you. You can find ways to conquer your loneliness. You can become each others' cures.

These steps will help lift you out of your doldrums so you can move on to learning from your experience.

Change Your Own Mind – And Your Life!

"Whatever you think you can do or believe you can do, begin it. Action has magic, grace and power in it."

This quote from Goethe, a statesman, scholar, artist

and man of the world, is a statement to the power of taking action. Let's face it: you can talk all day about what you are *going* to do, but it simply won't get done until you actually *do* it.

Sometimes being lonely can be fixed by simply changing your mind and deciding to not be lonely anymore. But how can that be? Psychologists say the messages you send out to others initiate within. In other words, how you feel inside is projected to the outside. In Sandra B.'s case, changing her mind changed a lot about her.

Sandra, a 42-year-old restaurant manager, was living a life that included work, going home, watching television, sleeping and doing the same thing all over again the next day. She had one or two close friends, including Meghan, her best friend since childhood and Connie, a lady she knew from work. She had no man in her life and openly claimed to not be looking for one at all. ("And that's perfectly okay with me because I don't have all the problems that men bring, thank you very much!" Sandra exclaimed.)

At this point in her life, Sandra did have a major "life problem" to deal with. Her mother, who lived across the country from her, was ill with cancer. As Sandra tried to deal with her mother's impending death and all the family business that was involved, she withdrew further and further into her little closed life.

After her mother finally passed away, Sandra dealt with her grief by seeing a therapist for several months. While she seemed to be doing well, she still felt down in the dumps. Her work was going well, but that was about it. Sandra's friend, Meghan, says: "I tried to get Sandi to go out with me on weekends. She rarely did and when she did, she always seemed to be anxious to leave not long after we got to where we were going. She almost seemed uncomfortable being in public and that was a surprise to me. She'd never been like that before."

Meghan and Connie both convinced Sandra to continue with her counseling in order to find out why she was becoming such a hermit. Through her work with her therapist, Sandra slowly but surely began to uncover some surprising facts about herself.

"I was extremely lonely! And the louder and more insistent I was that I didn't want or didn't need a man in my life, the worse I felt because it turned out I was just kidding myself," Sandra admits. "I really did want to be in a good, loving relationship. But the way I was living my life, I certainly wasn't going to end up in one."

Every now and then, Sandra got a phone call from Steve, a man she'd known for many years from a previous workplace. Steve had always been interested in Sandra, but Sandra had mixed feelings about Steve. She thought he wasn't her type, but she enjoyed his company and was good friends with him. They occasionally went out to dinner or for a drink and sometimes Steve came to Sandra's house for a home-cooked meal. If Sandra ever needed help with anything, all she had to do was call Steve and he'd be there, no matter what.

Now that Sandra realized how lonely she was, she began to look at Steve with different eyes. After so many years, could it be possible that the perfect man for her was right under her nose the whole time?

"I really started to wonder!" Sandra says. "Meghan and Connie both thought Steve and I would be the perfect couple. I was never that sure. But over a period of several months, something started to happen and Steve suddenly became a prospect for me."

As Sandra thought more and more of opening herself up to a relationship, her view of everything in the world around her changed. She did lots of work in her journal and one night, she wrote:

"Now is the time. I'm ready. I'd been lying to myself for a long time and I'm not going to do that anymore. I know that now I'm ready to bring someone into my life. And I can admit to myself – and to the world – that I'm ready to have someone in my life.

"No more loneliness. No more pain. I know someone is out there for me and now that I'm ready, he's going to find me. From now on, I'm living my life differently. I'm living it for me because I deserve a good life and I deserve a good man who loves me. And that's what I'm going to have."

It wasn't just Sandra's written words, though. She really had made up her mind and her conviction was obvious. Everybody around her noticed.

"Even I noticed that suddenly Sandi was, shall we say, more approachable," Meghan recalls.

"Before, I couldn't be sure what kind of mood she'd be in. It had gotten to a point where even I wasn't sure I could approach her at any given time. I'd sort of hang back and wait to see what her mood was. But after she changed, there was a warmth about her that just about radiated. In fact, it almost felt like it drew me in, attracted me to her. It was really amazing and I remember saying to her: 'What have you done to yourself? There's something different, but I can't put my finger on it!'"

Sandra replied to Meghan: "I've had a major attitude adjustment."

The "new" Sandra didn't escape Steve. One night, as Steve was dropping Sandra off after taking her out to dinner, everything just came together. Sandra knew that she wanted to give Steve a chance.

And Steve, who had all but given up hope that Sandra would ever want him in that way, was astounded. Their chemistry was so right and so strong that after one week, they felt as if they'd been together for a long, long time. After a year, they're still together, happier than ever and planning their future together.

Meghan was thrilled; Connie was skeptical at first. But after the couple had been together a year, she had to admit that it was working.

"I never would have thought that changing her mind about being lonely could literally change Sandra's life," Connie says. "But I saw it with my own eyes!"

It worked for Sandra – and it can work for you! Here's how:

1. Decide that you want to change your life. *Really* decide. "It's like going on a diet or quitting smoking," Sandra explains. "You have to mean it and really make a commitment to your decision."

2. Write it down. Create a sort of "mission statement" about your decision. Write down what it is you're doing and what you want to accomplish. For example, it could be not to be lonely any more, to open yourself up to the possibilities of love and to bring a loving relationship into your life.

3. Now write down why it's going to happen. Most of all, list all the reasons you deserve to not be lonely any more. For example: "I'm now ready for someone in my life and I know he'll find me because it's my time now. Good things happen to me, and I attract only good things and good luck."

4. Read what you've written every morning when you get up and every night before you go to bed. The more you read it, the more you'll believe in it and feel the changes happening in your life.

And don't forget, be sure to tell your friends and family that you're looking. This way, they can help you meet people. But you may not have to say a word. Your look and attitude will tell the world that you've changed your mind and are changing your life!

Raise Your Self-Esteem

What is self-esteem? Most experts say that it's a person's sense of self-worth, a feeling they have of being valuable. The person likes herself and is happy with herself. She feels she is okay in the world.

Says psychologist Doris Wild Helmering, in a February 27, 1993 *St. Louis Post-Dispatch* article: "Some people seem to have had high self-esteem all their lives. As far back as they can remember, they liked themselves. Others can recall only feeling bad about themselves."

Most of us, says Helmering, go through cycles where our self-esteem goes up and down relative to ongoing events in our lives. "Poor health, job loss, marital problems, inability to lose weight and not being able to pay bills generally lower self-esteem," she says in the article. "A promotion, a happy marriage, a signed contract, a new hairstyle or a clean house may increase one's self-esteem."

Low self-esteem can keep you lonely. The message you're sending to other people is the same message you give to yourself: I'm not worthy. I'm not valuable.

If others are getting this message from you, they'll certainly avoid you!

Luckily, most people can improve their self-esteem. And the way to feel better, says Helmering, is to ask yourself what would make you feel more valuable. Then set goals toward achieving that. Says Helmering: "When people set and pursue goals, their self-esteem grows."

We must be careful, however, not to seek our value in others. It's not good to say that if you have a relationship, you'll be a better, more worthy person. You have to feel that you're valuable before you can attract someone into your life!

Let's look at ways to improve your self-esteem and examine how women and their relationships are affected by low self-esteem.

Something's Wrong With Me

Psychotherapist Emily Hancock, author of the book *The Girl Within,* works with lonely women in her clinical practice. In a February 1994 *Cosmopolitan* magazine, Hancock referred to a study conducted by Harvard professor Carol Gilligan. Women and men were both shown flash cards of solitary figures. Incredibly, the women felt a sense of fear and impending danger when they saw the cards, while the men did not. Other pictures showing people placed far apart had totally different effects on men and women: Women were disturbed by the images. Men were threatened by pictures showing people in close contact.

Said Hancock in the *Cosmopolitan* article: "Women feel strange and, very often, defective if they're unpaired."

Defective? Because you don't have a relationship in your life!?! No wonder women can feel such low self-esteem and lack of self-worth! No wonder they can sabotage themselves when they want to have good, loving relationships! And often our culture pushes that message on women – through television shows, movies, advertising and other images.

Do any of these sentences describe you?

❖ I'd be happier in a different job, but I can't change.

❖ If I had a boyfriend (husband, baby), I'd be happy.

❖ If I had more friends, I'd go out more.

❖ If I had someone to dress up for, I would.

If you think thoughts such as these, you are looking to others to feel good about yourself when what you should be doing is looking to yourself for self-esteem. Don't rely on the approval of others to make you feel good about yourself. But most importantly, don't think that being part of a couple is the only thing that makes you a worthwhile person. Because if you do, the crushing blow you deliver to your own self-esteem can actually be one of the primary things that keeps someone from entering your life!

In recent years, the term "self-esteem" has become almost a buzzword in many ways. Yet that lack of self-esteem is truly the root of so many dysfunctional relationships – or people who have trouble forming any relationships at all.

Where Does Low Self-Esteem Come From?

Psychologists agree that low self-esteem begins in childhood. If your parents praised you for things you did well and in general gave you positive messages about yourself, you would learn to regard yourself highly. But if they didn't do this and provided you with negative messages about yourself instead, you could suffer from a great lack of self-confidence as an adult. It's this lack of self-confidence that can keep you alone, since you feel no one could possibly love or want you.

This doesn't mean low self-esteem *always* comes from childhood. Sometimes, we just go through bad times in our lives that affect us more strongly than we might have thought. The strong imprints of these bad times can also cause us to think less of ourselves and the more we do it, the better we become at putting ourselves down.

How can you turn negative messages from your childhood – or your adulthood – into positive ones? By looking to experiences you've had in the present and using them to increase your confidence, experts say.

Alma used to think no one would ever want her because she had small breasts. "My older brothers always teased me, even when I was 16 years old," she recalls. "They called me 'Ironing board Alma,' and I could still hear their taunting voices echoing through my mind 20 years later.

"It wasn't until I was nearly 40 that I met a wonderful man who thought my figure was just perfect. He felt that my smaller bust was far more attractive than larger ones. He made me feel so wonderful, I finally began to like myself just the way I was. The more he complimented me – and loved me – the less I could hear my brother's voices."

In a February 1989 *Cosmopolitan* article, New York psychotherapist JoAnn Magdoff says that liking yourself more comes from "learning to let in the nice things other people say to you – the praise from unexpected sources. There are small increments of good feelings that are given to you in the course of a day or a week that if you don't feel good about yourself, you tend to just discount."

So anyone who pays you a compliment should be thanked and the compliment should be taken at face value. "Don't analyze it, don't criticize it, don't put the person down," says Magdoff in the article. "These positive connections, even in the smallest ways, are little building blocks of self-esteem."

Alma believed she was somehow physically deficient, but women can also believe they are lacking in other ways: intelligence, charm, worldliness, even mechanical ability (yes, men do like women who can fix things around the house!). What can counteract this thinking? Magdoff says to take specific actions that can make you feel like a fuller, better person. In the *Cosmopolitan* article, she suggests boosting your self-confidence by:

- Doing volunteer work. Teach literacy classes, for example, and feel better about your life.

- Extending your skills. Learn to speak another language or take up a complex sport such as horseback riding. Activities such as these, Magdoff says, can enhance your sense of self and thus your power to attract others to you.

Don't Look For Self-Worth In Other People

Women with low self-esteem often try to prove their self-worth through other people, according to Dr. William Larrison, a Florida counselor. In an article in the *Palm*

Beach Post, Dr. Larrison describes Nancy, a nurse who feels defective, inadequate and worthless.

"Nancy lives with an internal critic who says things like, 'Nobody really likes you. You are not worth caring for. Why do you even look for love?'" writes Dr. Larrison. "Yet Nancy also feels desperate without a man in her life. 'I am nobody unless I have somebody,' she has told me again and again. In one of her most lucid moments, she has said, 'If I can get a man to love me, then maybe I won't feel so unlovable.'"

So what is the answer for people like Nancy who want to raise their self-esteem? According to Dr. Larrison, there is no shortcut or quick fix answer if you suffer from a lifetime of self-doubt and self-criticism. Low self-esteem doesn't develop overnight and it won't be fixed overnight, either.

"The first step is to recognize what we are doing to ourselves," wrote Larrison. You can become so used to the critical, condemning messages you give yourselves that they feel normal.

Next, writes Larrison, you should write down the negative assumptions that you have about yourself. This brings to light the dark thoughts we have about ourselves. Now, you can learn to talk back to the negative thoughts and develop a sense of yourself that is more realistic.

"Remember, just because we feel inadequate, it doesn't mean that we *are* inadequate," Larrison writes. "Our feelings do not determine our worth. With a more objective and kinder stance, our assumptions about ourselves will begin to change. We will feel better, our self-esteem will be boosted, our sense of worthlessness and depression will begin to disappear."

Self-Acceptance – Learn It!

One of the keys to finding your perfect dance partner is to learn to like yourself – and to accept your faults. It's all part of who you are. You've probably heard it said a millions times: How can anyone else possibly love you if you can't love yourself? And the reason you've heard it so many times is that it's true!

Self-acceptance isn't always easy, however, and one thing that can hold you back is an inability to get past your faults if you haven't dealt with them or can't deal with them. If this happens, experts suggest you try to find something to love about your faults.

You can like yourself better and find ways to love your faults if you "treat yourself like you would a beloved friend," says Dr. David Burns, a Philadelphia psychiatrist, director of the Institute for Cognitive and Behavioral Therapies and author of the books *Intimate Connections* and *Feeling Good*. In a February 1989 *Cosmopolitan* article, Burns said: Give yourself the kind of positive, reassuring, compassionate messages you would give a friend."

Most of us have trouble saying positive things to ourselves. We can feel embarrassed, goofy, silly or just plain weird if we try to say, "I'm a good person and I deserve good things in my life." Yet we find it very easy to say awful, negative things to ourselves. Words such as "Gee, I'm always doing such stupid things, no wonder no one likes me" roll off our tongues as if we were born saying them.

If we were half as good at positive self-talk as we are at negative self-talk, we would have far fewer problems in life! Learn to get very good at positive self-talk by practicing. Listen for all the times you say negative things to yourself and immediately correct the thoughts with positive ones. For example:

You're walking into a party and you catch yourself thinking: "I'm dressed all wrong again! My clothes are ugly and all the women will notice and laugh at me and the men will think I'm just some backward girl who doesn't know how to dress right."

Pretend you're with a friend who had those feelings instead and voiced them out loud to you. What would you say to your friend? You'd probably say:

"But your hair looks great! And nobody can dance like you. And your personality can win over anyone in the room!" Treat yourself as well as you'd treat that imaginary friend. Tell yourself those positive things, then walk into the room with great self-confidence.

This trick has always worked for Linda, but she never did it consciously. Linda truly did love herself just the way she was, including her extra 75 pounds. Linda had several friends who were also overweight, but none of them could attract a man like Linda could. Why? None of them had Linda's self-confidence.

Linda says: "I've spent my life dieting, losing pounds, putting them back on, only to lose them again and gain them back one more time. I have two entirely different wardrobes for my two different weights. But back in my late 20s, I came to a realization that just because I had two weights and two wardrobes didn't mean I had to have two different personalities.

"I could have a happy, cheery, self-confident personality (the thinner one) and a mopey, sad, depressed, hate-myself personality (the heavier one) – *if* I let myself! But once I realized this, I didn't have two personalities anymore. I chose to accept my flaw and work with it. Or, in reality, to ignore it and let the rest of me shine through."

It always worked. Linda usually had several men vying for her attention at the same time. But her friends rarely had anyone. Linda could hear her friends putting themselves down, out loud, to other people!

"It almost makes me cry when I see and hear how badly my friends put themselves down," she says. "I've told them to stop it, to start praising themselves and to find something to like about themselves. But so far, only one friend has made any progress in raising her self-esteem. I try to help them. But they can't be helped if they don't want it, either."

Self-confidence can bring people to you – men and women – because of the subtle messages you put forth to them. If you believe that you are a worthy person, a good person, attractive and fun to be with, this is the message you project and others pick up on.

Likewise, lack of self-confidence can push people away from you. If you don't feel good about yourself, you project this outwardly for other people to pick up on. You have to ask yourself: If I don't like myself very much, how can others like me? This is something that can keep you from forming the very type of relationship you seek.

Show Compassion – For Yourself!

You probably consider yourself a compassionate person. You feel for others who are in trouble and try to help whenever you can. You strive to be patient and understanding with people you meet. You generally can forgive other people their faults and mistakes and you don't expect unreasonable things from them. Compassion – it's part of who you are, your personality and the true inner you.

Then why in the world can't you feel any compassion for yourself?

If you start treating yourself with compassion, your self-esteem will improve, say Dr. Matthew McKay, Ph.D. and Patrick Fanning in their book *Self-Esteem*.

"The essence of self-esteem is compassion for yourself," they write. "When you have compassion for yourself, you understand and accept yourself. If you make a mistake, you forgive yourself. You have reasonable expectations of yourself. You set attainable goals. You tend to see yourself as basically good."

When you feel compassion for yourself, McKay and Fanning write, you can find your own sense of worth. It's like discovering a buried treasure! Compassionate self-talk, they say, can wash away the sediment of hurt and rejection that may have covered your innate self-acceptance for years.

Compassion lets you forgive your mistakes and preserve your self-esteem. You maintain your sense of self-worth and pride.

Now, let's take a reality-check:

- Write down the five most important people in your life. Write them down in order of importance, from one to five.

- Look at who number one is on the list. Is it you? If not, why not? Could it be that you're waiting for someone else to make you number one?

You probably cringed at the idea that you should have written yourself down as number one on the list. Why? Because doing so would be selfish or vain?

Placing yourself on the list, experts say, is *not* selfish, but rather is a sign of someone who has positive self-esteem.

Journaling For Self-Esteem

A great way to know yourself better – and build up your self-esteem in the process – is through journaling. By taking some time each day for yourself to write in your personal journal, you can begin to find all the reasons for liking yourself that you can't seem to find right now! The trick with journaling is to find all the negative things you say about yourself and even negative things that you do and turn them around to positives.

"The spirit is indomitable. There can be something positive in every situation," says Dr. Lila Swell, a psychologist and author of the book *Success: You Can Make It Happen*. In her book, she writes: "You must take control of those parts of your life that are possible for you to control. Progress comes from directed, purposeful action."

That action is to begin journaling. Start the first few days by:

♣ Exploring your strengths and reminding yourself of them. "A strength is any talent, ability, skill or positive personal trait that you use and that contributes to your growth and productivity," says Dr. Swell. Think back in your life and make a list of the strengths you developed as a result of your childhood and your past experiences, and list what good things came from them. Knowing your strengths can make you feel better about yourself.

Many of us have been taught that to say we are good at something is wrong. But we are rarely discouraged from putting ourselves down. This is wrong, writes Dr. Swell. We need to know what our strengths are in order to raise our own self-esteem. "Strength is power. Your strengths will set you free. Confidence comes from seeing your real strengths."

♣ Write down the things you dislike most about your job, your living situation, your clothes — anything at all in your life. Take one subject at a time. Now ask yourself: Is this something I can change for the good? If so, then do it! You may be surprised at how simple it is to change some things that have been making you feel bad.

If you can't change something you don't like, however, devise some strategies to cope with the situation. Find ways to gradually learn to accept what you can't change and think positively about it in that way. Another trick is to make the thing you dislike insignificant in the overall picture. Additionally, make yourself bigger than what you don't like. How can it possibly bother you then!

It all boils down to perspective. The way you view things can affect how you view yourself. This is where the next two tips will help you tremendously in boosting your self-esteem.

♣ Use your journal to list your past successes in all aspects of your life. Sometimes, just putting these positive things about yourself down on paper will brighten your attitude considerably!

Include things from your childhood through adulthood, anything in which you accomplished something you were proud of: winning at sports or a spelling bee in high school; cooking a fabulous gourmet meal; raising a child who's a good student in school, or taking perfect photographs.

Once you have your list (and keep adding to it as you remember things day after day), you can always look back on it to remind yourself that you have accomplished things in the past and you can do so again. This alone can do wonders for a sagging self-esteem.

♣ Write down thoughts you have about yourself, then rate the thought as either positive or negative. Examine the thought again and ask yourself: Is this thought the truth? You'll be interested to learn that thinking truthfully, rather than positively or negatively, can raise your self-esteem. People whose self-esteem is strong have the ability to see situations as they really are, factually and truthfully.

If you use your journaling to learn to do this, you'll become someone who isn't afraid of the truth, someone who is confident enough in yourself to face the reality of things. To develop this ability, simply ask yourself regularly: "Is what I'm thinking true?" And if it isn't, examine the situation again. This technique can help you gain a new perspective on your situation and lead toward attitude change.

More Ways To Make Journaling Work For You

Keeping a positive attitude is one way to even out the bumpy road. You can build a positive attitude by working with positive affirmations. It's a form of self-talk, a way of working down to your deepest thoughts and fears and replacing them with positive, uplifting messages about yourself and your life.

It's easy to work with affirmations and it can be a lot of fun, too! Just create some positive messages for and about yourself and each day write them down. Several times a day, read the affirmations. You can read them out loud if you wish. The more you write and read them, the more you reinforce the positive messages in your mind.

Here are some positive affirmations that you might begin with:

❖ I am a good person and I deserve love.

❖ I am worthy of being loved.

❖ I am open to receiving love into my life.

❖ I am capable of giving love in return.

❖ I find true goodness and love within myself.

❖ Others sense my true nature and are open to receiving me in their lives.

Whether you write these affirmations down or say them out loud, pay attention to what happens next. Do you find yourself getting a bit uncomfortable from saying such nice things about yourself? This is your internal critic trying to give you negative messages. Don't listen to it!

When you hear the negative critic inside you, write down what it's saying, then turn down the volume. Look carefully at what the critic says about you. Ask yourself: Is it true? Is it real? Then take the negative thought and re-write it as a positive one. Do this with everything your inner critic says about you.

You *can* defeat your negative inner critic if you keep at it and practice!

Practice by first using the affirmations suggested on the previous page. Listen to the negative messages you get and write them down, then write more affirmations to counteract them.

For example, if you say that you are worthy of being loved and your inner critic says back to you: "I don't think so or you'd have someone in your life loving you right now – and you don't!" you can create a new affirmation that says: "My self-worth is not tied to other people. I'm still worthy of being loved."

Add these new affirmations to the list above and work with them every day. You'll be surprised at how soon you can believe these positive messages and how quickly your whole attitude will change for the better.

Monitor Your Judgmental Self

For three days, write down all the negative things your inner critic says about you throughout the day. At the end of the day, put the list in your journal so you can examine it better. Read the criticisms and ask yourself what action they want you to take. A criticism will either want you to:

✔ Do something good, or

✔ Stop doing something bad.

Make a note after each criticism and soon you will begin to see a pattern. You'll find that you're probably setting very high – if not impossible – standards for yourself. Standards that virtually no one could meet. By forcing these standards on yourself, you set yourself up for disappointment when you can't live up to the perfectionism you demand from yourself. In this way, you feel less sure of yourself and your self-esteem suffers.

By studying these things your inner critic says each day, you can combat them with positive, reality-based responses.

"I Get No Respect!"

When your self-esteem is low, others sense this. And sometimes you may not get a lot of respect as a result. This is what happened to Ginnie W., a 41-year-old divorced mother of two:

"For years, I thought no one respected me," she says. "I was a homemaker for most of my life and when I got divorced three years ago, I had to wake up really fast to the fact that now I was on my own. I had to take care of myself completely.

"The problem was, my self-esteem was in the pits from the divorce. I was convinced that since my husband no longer wanted me, no one else would ever want me, either. When I had to go out to work as a secretary in order to feed my kids, I felt my bosses and even my co-workers didn't respect me. And you know what? They didn't! Because I felt so badly about myself, I wasn't doing anything to earn anyone else's respect! It took me a while to find that out.

"I worked with my therapist on my self-esteem issues and along with that I learned some things to do to face the people at work and strive to win their respect.

It didn't happen overnight. After a while, I was able to make them feel differently about me – but *only* after I felt differently about myself!"

As your self-esteem recovers, you'll notice other people treating you with more respect. Ginnie's poor self-esteem was a contributing factor to her bosses and co-workers not treating her with respect.

According to professor of counseling Dr. Samuel Gladding, we first have to respect ourselves and be comfortable with who we are in order to win respect from others.

"Respect is something you earn – it's not something that just happens," said Dr. Gladding. Earning respect takes time and effort, he said. It's something you have to work for, but it's definitely worth striving for.

Here are some of the strategies Ginnie used to gain the respect of others, as well as some tips from Dr. Gladding:

1. Make direct eye contact with people. People like to be acknowledged in a conversation and one way we can do that is by making eye contact with them. You show that you're involved in the conversation psychologically and physically and it shows that you're confident of yourself. If you're confident of yourself, others will sense that and return respect. Self-confident people will always earn respect.

2. Be appropriate in how you treat other people. Whether it's your boss, your assistant or your buddy, you win respect by treating other people as though they have dignity and worth. From the bottom up or top down, letting people know they count is important.

3. Adopt a personal policy of honesty. Those people we admire most are truthful people, such as Abraham Lincoln, who we call "Honest Abe." Even if we don't like what is said, people like to be told the truth as long as it's done without bludgeoning. Others respect an honest and truthful person. But be sure you're tactful when being honest, of course. Honesty will always earn respect.

4. Be yourself with others. That way, people won't think you're putting on airs and they'll respect you for it. Most people can spot a phony pretty quickly and phonies get no respect at all.

5. Don't be a know-it-all. If you're starting a new job and don't know something, for example, ask for help from someone who does know. Don't pretend you know something if you don't. And don't pretend you know *everything* because no one does. It makes you more approachable if you're not a know-it-all. People respect someone they can talk to, rather than someone who talks to them all the time.

6. Stay on top of current events. To be conversational, you need knowledge of what's happening in the world. If you have an opinion on a subject, for example, you're likely to be asked why you hold that opinion. If your answer is, "I don't know," you come across as completely uninformed. People respect someone who is up-to-date on things.

7. Be open to the opinions of others. People aren't enthralled with others who are dogmatic, but they do respect and enjoy the company of those who have some knowledge yet are open to learning more. People who think they are right all the time and everyone else is wrong will never earn any respect. It shows you're narrow-minded and intolerant. Open-mindedness is a quality that earns respect.

8. Be prompt when others are expecting you at a certain time. We respect people who do what they say they're going to do. We admire those who start and end things on time and those who make a point of being somewhere when they say they're going to be. It shows that you have respect for other people's time and you aren't going to keep them sitting around wasting their time, drumming their fingers and waiting for you.

9. Maintain a neat and appropriate appearance. This shows you really do care about yourself. You don't have to wear expensive clothing to win respect, but you do need to have a clean, neat appearance that shows people you respect yourself, your body and your clothes. Appropriate means that you wouldn't want to go to a business meeting in blue jeans, unless your business calls for that. Be aware of what kind of dress different situations call for and respond sensitively and sensibly. Also, be aware of how you carry yourself and do so with pride. When you stand and walk with good posture, you create a positive image that people respond to.

10. Communicate clearly with others. Be specific about what you want or need. That way people know more about you and can therefore respond better to you. If you're not clear when you communicate with others, they're left to guess what you're talking about. People aren't mind-readers and expecting them to be doesn't build respect.

11. Do something nice for someone. Do charity work or contribute to a good cause. Help someone who needs help, even if it's something small, like giving directions to a lost out-of-towner or picking up a package someone dropped at the supermarket. This shows you're not self-centered and it betters your community in the bargain. People aren't enthralled with others who are self-centered.

12. Use humor in your daily life. People respect others who can both laugh at themselves and laugh at a situation. Not everything is dead-serious, so keep a perspective on what really is important and be able to laugh with people and certainly not at them.

As you work on raising your own self-esteem, watch how other people treat you. You'll see a big difference as they sense that you are feeling tip-top about yourself! Now that you're feeling better, let's work on feeling comfortable being alone.

Feel Comfortable By Yourself

Have you ever known someone who wasn't comfortable with him- or herself? Are you like that?

Marianne, a 39-year-old nurse from Los Angeles, was absolutely convinced that she was no one without a man. When she broke up with a boyfriend, it rarely took her longer than a few days to pick up someone else. And the longer she engaged in this behavior, the more destructive it became, according to Marianne's sister, Lisa.

"Marianne did this for many years. Each time, she seemed to pick up another man more quickly than before," says Lisa. "This usually meant one thing: She knew less and less about these guys. And each time, she picked up someone who was more incompatible with her than the last bozo."

Lisa was distraught with her sister's behavior and spent a lot of time trying to talk some sense into her. But Marianne wouldn't listen.

"I tried to get her to see that she needed to slow down, recover from her broken relationships and put herself back together," recalls Lisa. "But she didn't see it. She was so frightened of being alone, of being unloved. Basically, she panicked."

What Marianne didn't realize is that, in her panic,

she oozed a look and feel of desperation. This was easily picked up on by men with less than honorable intentions.

"They latched onto her. They knew they could take advantage of her," says Lisa. "It got worse. Finally, it backfired on her, but by that time, I was afraid it was too late."

Marianne got involved with a man who verbally and emotionally abused her. He sensed her low self-esteem and used it on his own power trip, but not before he made Marianne believe she was the love of his life. Then came the bombshell discovery.

"The skunk was married and had three kids!" Lisa exclaims. "Marianne found out when she got suspicious one night about something Mark told her and she decided to follow him after work. That's when she learned about his family and later found that he and his wife had been going through serious problems for years and years. But he had her under his thumb, too, and she couldn't leave him. So he continued to abuse her, all the while living whatever life he chose — and ruining however many women's lives he wanted to. Including my sister's."

Lisa was finally able to convince Marianne to get professional help. Marianne began seeing a therapist and worked hard to overcome her discomfort at being alone. And she learned that she kept repeating her relationship mistakes because she never took the time to become comfortable with herself. She believed she wasn't "complete" unless she had a man. Where did this belief come from?

"A lot of this belief came from other people," Lisa explains. "Our mother, for example, was always harassing her: 'When are you going to get married? Am I ever going to have grandchildren? How come you don't have a nice man yet?' The older Marianne got, the more our mother pushed at her. It certainly had an effect on Marianne."

The effect was to make Marianne reckless in her pursuit of a man – *any* man.

"I was *so* desperate, I'd take anyone," Marianne admits. "I couldn't bear to listen to my mother anymore or my friends who were always on my case, too. All my friends were married and, frankly, I think they felt uncomfortable being friends with me because I was single. It's almost like they were afraid I'd steal one of their husbands or something."

It's obvious Marianne didn't get much help from her friends as far as becoming comfortable with herself. But working with her therapist, she was able to slow down, relax and take some time to really get to know herself so she could be comfortable being alone with herself. One of the first things Marianne had to do was know – and accept – that it's perfectly okay to be alone, even in a world that seems to be made for couples.

Why Being Alone Is OK

You probably know some women who are single, living alone and very happy with their lives. And you've probably noticed that they attract plenty of people into their lives. Have you ever wondered why, particularly if you're so unhappy being alone?

These women are making the most of being alone. They have learned to enjoy being by themselves – and with themselves. Here are what some women say about their lives alone:

❧ "I'm free to concentrate on my career because I'm alone. The only person I ever have to really answer to is myself."

❧ "I have a great job and make plenty of money. I don't have any reason to 'settle' for any man just because he can take care of me. I'm leaving myself open for true love. Right now, I can take care of myself perfectly fine, thank you!"

❧ "Hey, I figure I can either enjoy being alone or be miserable. I've never been one to be miserable, so I'm enjoying the heck out of being alone!"

In the January 11, 1998 issue of *Psychology Today*, Dr. Ester Buchholz, a developmental psychologist, writes: "Meaningful alonetime, it turns out, is a powerful need and a necessary tonic in today's rapid-fire world. Indeed, solitude actually allows us to connect to others in a far richer way."

How is this? Buchholz writes that we mistakenly believe aloneness and attachment to be an either/or condition, when in reality, they go together and one enriches the other. For this reason, she implores us all to "discover the joys of solitude."

There are indeed great benefits to being alone, says Brian Greer, M.D., a psychiatrist, and Carla Greer, a psychologist. If you look at these benefits and learn to appreciate them, you can become more comfortable with your situation and be better poised to bring another person into your life.

"Know that your best chance for meeting someone who is good for you will be when you can feel happy and confident on your own," the Greers write in their book *Why Women Get the Blues* (American Media, Inc.) "You end up conveying something non-verbally that will draw people to you like a magnet."

Here are some tips from the Greers and other experts on how to be happy being alone:

✔ Form strong ties with others. Just because you live alone doesn't mean you can't have close relationships. You may have to work a bit harder to form those ties, though.

"Personal contact in which we feel understood and accepted – there's no more powerful gift," says Ken Druck, a San Diego psychologist who specializes in working with singles, in an article in the August 3, 1987 issue of *U.S. News & World Report*. "If this need isn't met, it translates into health problems and hampers success."

✔ Spend a lot of time improving and pampering yourself. In doing so, your health will benefit, you'll look and feel better, and your mind will become sharper. Start an exercise program, cook healthy meals for yourself, meditate and practice yoga. Create your own healthy lifestyle.

✔ Pursue your interests, hobbies and dreams with full force since your time is really your own. Take classes that interest you and develop your mind. Make a list of things you've always wanted to do but never did. Now is the time to do them!

✔ Turn your home into your own private haven, your corner of the world that is safe and nurturing. Create an atmosphere that feeds your heart and soul.

✔ Give time to your friends and create a strong support system. Be there for them when they have problems and they'll be there for you when you need help. Many people who are alone think of their circle of friends as a surrogate family. Try to make these unconditional relationships, where you can be there for each other without having to get something from each other in return.

✔ Get involved with projects that reflect your values and beliefs. Join your church charity groups or pick a civic project that you believe in and donate your time. Along the way, you'll meet plenty of like-minded people. You can gain a great sense of belonging by associating with people who share your interests and beliefs.

Find Out Who You Are

If you had to live with a complete stranger for even a short period of time, would you be completely comfortable with that? Probably not! You would want to take some time to get to know the person so he or she wouldn't BE a stranger any longer. The more you learned about the persons likes, dislikes, beliefs and feelings, the more comfortable you would become living with them. Unfamiliar territory can carry hidden dangers and risks, but familiar territory is easy to navigate. It makes all the difference in the world.

Do you know who *you* are? It may seem like an odd question, but experts say that people who aren't comfortable being alone with themselves may simply not know themselves very well. It isn't much of a stretch to compare the two situations. If you don't know yourself too well, it may make you uncomfortable when you're alone. So the next step to being comfortable alone is to get to know yourself a bit better.

Women especially have a tendency to think, "Someone loves me, so I must be all right." You can see where there might be a problem if the woman doesn't have a relationship. She can assume that she's not "all right" without another person. It certainly helps to think back over your life and see that you indeed have had a life, even if there wasn't another person in it all the time.

So who are you anyway? You may be surprised to find that you don't even know anymore! Try some of these soul-searching exercises to help you dig up information about yourself that will help you become more self-confident being alone.

What Do I Need? What Do I Want?

One of the reasons why women aren't comfortable being alone is that they feel their needs aren't being met. But can they really say that they know what their needs are? Not always! In fact, we tend to confuse our needs with our wants — and there is a big difference between the two.

Experts say that our needs are the most basic forces that motivate us. Our wants, on the other hand, are things we may desire, but don't require our immediate attention and satisfaction. If we confuse the two, we may be spending a lot of time going after things we want, while our true needs suffer. When our needs aren't fulfilled, we continue to be unhappy and do not have a sense of what is really necessary to our lives. And if we know the difference, we can satisfy our own needs more often than you might believe.

Perhaps this is why we remain lonely. We don't realize that connections with people aren't just things we want, but are things we need. Because of this, they should be priorities in our lives.

Relationship therapist Dr. Gilda Carle addressed

this topic in her book *Don't Bet On The Prince: How To Have The Man You Want By Betting On Yourself*. She writes that women must know their needs in order to be happy with themselves.

"So many women think they need a man, but the truth is they want a man. Not knowing the difference is what keeps them running headlong into any relationship that makes itself available and that usually results in disaster," Dr. Carle writes. "Realizing that you can satisfy your own needs – and a man is not a need – will lead you to becoming your own person again and make you more open to a good relationship with a man that you want. Just knowing this difference can give you a big attitude shift."

Begin to take care of your needs immediately. Your wants can wait until you feel more comfortable being with yourself. Going on a search for what exactly your wants and needs are is a big step to learning more about yourself.

It may surprise you to discover that your needs are few, but your wants are great. This is great news! Things you want can be obtained later. Get into your needs first – find out what basics are necessary to survive and leave the wants for later.

Ask yourself: What do I need in my life? Your list might look like this:

1. Money for food, shelter, clothing, transportation

2. My job

3. My family's support

4. Friends

5. Exercise and good food to stay healthy

6. My hobby/interest (photography, reading, sewing, painting, etc.) to enrich and occupy me

Does it surprise you that, once you put your mind to really defining what you need, your needs don't take very long to write down? When you look at the short list, you realize that it should be easier to take care of your needs than you might have believed.

Next, you should list your wants. The purpose of this is not to make getting things that you want a driving force in your life, but rather to see all the things your mind can be occupied with – and confusing with needs. Once you have this list, you should prioritize your wants according to what's most important for you to express your passions.

For example, maybe you've always wanted to learn to play the piano or you want the latest hot new sports car. Decide which has higher priority for you and then go for it first. You may notice that some of your wants are things you've been missing because you didn't give much time to yourself as a person. All the more reason to go for them now, to reinforce your individual identity and find out who you really are.

Learn More About Yourself

Do you know what your greatest strength is? Your biggest weakness? Do you remember what your favorite comfort food was as a child? Did eating that food go a long way toward making you feel better if you were ill or feeling blue?

There are many things you may not know about yourself and many more things you do know, but have forgotten or written off as old childhood "stuff." Sometimes, going back into childhood "stuff" and doing these things again as an adult can make you feel more connected to the real you, the uninhibited child-like you.

Here are some exercises designed to make you think back in your life and pull up memories about the person you are seeking – yourself. Complete these sentences in the journal you've been using for self-esteem building. If you feel the urge to write more about the topic than just filling in the blanks, do it! You can discover even more about yourself by doing "stream of consciousness" writing on a topic. Just put pen to paper and let it flow.

1. When I was a child, my mother/father used to read to me the story/book _____.

2. My most favorite toy as a kid was _____.

3. I'll never forget going to see the movie _____. I can still remember the scene that impressed me the most, when

   _____.

4. I learned to play the musical instrument _____ when I was a kid. I also wanted to learn to play the_____.

5. As a child, my favorite book to read was

   _____.

6. My favorite child's game to play was

   _____.

7. If I was sick and stayed home from school, my

mother fed me _____ and it really made me feel better.

8. If I got good grades or behaved myself (or other accomplishment), my mother fed me _____ as a reward.

9. My most favorite piece of clothing as a child was _____.

10. My favorite place to ride my bicycle was _____.

11. If I wanted to be alone, I had a place to go where no grown-ups could find me. They never knew about it and it was my secret place all to myself. That place was located _____.

12. My secret place looked like _____.

13. When I was five years old, I wanted to be a _____ when I grew up.

14. When I was 10 years old, I wanted to be a _____ when I grew up.

15. When I was a child, I always wanted to _____, but never did.

16. When I was a child, I needed_____, but didn't have it.

17. When I was a child, I really wanted a_____, but didn't get it.

18. My favorite TV show was_____. My favorite TV character was_____.

This exercise helps to dig up information about yourself that you can use to learn how to be more comfortable with yourself. For example, what did you want to be when you were ten years old? Is there anything about your answer that you can do now, just for fun? Suppose you wanted to be a police officer. Your community may have a Citizen's Observer Patrol (COPs) program you could join – doing this, you can give some volunteer time to your community at the same time you "fulfill" a childhood fantasy.

Is there a musical instrument you wanted to learn to play? If you didn't do it, you might try it now. Accomplishing this long-buried goal can go a long way toward making you feel better about yourself.

Look at some other items: your favorite food, your favorite movie or TV show. These things made you feel better as a child. Can you use them now? Fix that favorite food for yourself when you're feeling a bit low, even if it's a peanut butter and banana sandwich!

What did you want as a child, but never got? Is it something you might get for yourself now? This might fill a void in your life that you had for years and years, but never realized it.

Can you still go visit your favorite secret place that no one knew about? Is it still there? Does it still look the same? The next time you're feeling low and need to get away by yourself, go to your favorite childhood secret place. You can get a lot of comfort from it, just as you did in the past.

You can learn a lot about yourself – new things and old things you may have forgotten – by working with the exercises above. Do put a lot of thought into the exercises and you'll come up with information that can really help you.

Wish Lists

Now, take a moment to find out what some of your dreams are in your life right now. Fill in the blanks in this "Wish List:"

1. I wish I could _____.

2. I wish I had _____.

3. I wish I could go _____.

4. I wish I didn't have to _____.

5. I wish I had more _____.

6. I wish I could stop _____.

7. I wish I could start_____.

8. I wish I had never _____.

9. I wish I had less _____.

10. I especially wish that I _____.

Look at your Wish List. This list represents things you'd like to do or stop doing, things you regret, and things you want. It tells a lot about who you are. It's an interesting list that can now become a list of goals, things you can strive for. Pick one to work on and, depending on the degree of difficulty in achieving it, make it your goal for the week, month or even year.

Developing – And Keeping – A Positive Attitude

There are good days and there are bad days. One day you're on top of the world and the next day you're so far down in the dumps, you have to look up to see a grasshopper's knees. Why can't life get on a nice level track and stay there? Because you're still feeling your way out of your confusion, discovering who you really are. And any process of rebirth has its pains.

Keeping a positive attitude is one way to even out the bumpy road and get comfortable being alone. As you learned in the chapter on building self-esteem, you can build a positive attitude by working with positive affirmations. Use self-talk to create positive messages about being by yourself and with yourself, write them down each day and read them. Reinforce the message that it's okay for you to be alone and indeed you can gain a lot from getting the most out of being alone.

Here are some suggestions for affirmations:

❦ Being alone allows me to know myself better.

❦ Being alone brings me peace of mind.

❦ I can better prepare myself to bring someone into my life by being alone for a while.

❦ Being alone makes me strong and independent.

❦ Being alone builds my character.

❦ I am comfortable being alone because I like myself and enjoy my own company.

Keep Busy By Volunteering Your Time And Services

A great way to keep yourself busy while meeting new people and raising your own self-esteem is to get into volunteer work. It's also a good way to put your own life into perspective.

If you're feeling down about yourself – or feeling lonely – the work you do to help others less fortunate than yourself will show how much you really DO have in your life and how lucky you are to have it.

Volunteering is a give-and-take situation: You give of your time and of yourself to others and you can take back a great feeling of accomplishment and self-worth. What could be better!

If you've simply written a check in the past to a good cause, try giving your time to the cause. It's a wonderful self-esteem booster. Here are just a few ideas for volunteer work:

❖ Help children by tutoring at a local school. Most schools have volunteer tutoring programs and are actively seeking qualified people. Pick a subject related to your work or your interests and specialties. Inner-city schools and even some overcrowded suburban schools are in special need of tutors.

❖ Work at a senior center. Spending time with lonely older people can help you alleviate your own loneliness. Visit for a chat and coffee or tea; play cards or shuffleboard with them; bring a book or magazine and read out loud. Most anything you do will make someone feel very special, just because you took the time to spend with them.

❈ Volunteer at an animal shelter. Play with puppies and kittens, walk dogs and if you're a true animal lover, clean cages and feed the animals. Shelters are usually very needy of volunteers and will welcome your compassionate assistance.

❈ Get involved with organized activities, such as the Special Olympics and fund raisers for other charity organizations. Special events such as these are always time-consuming and organizers are always looking for help. Plan a 10K run for charity or perhaps a local telethon. There's no shortage of worthy charities needing your help in this regard.

❈ Love the great outdoors? Volunteer to be a guide at a nature center, zoo or park. If you enjoy being outdoors and know something about nature or are interested in learning, you can share your knowledge with others while being out in the environment.

❈ If indoors is more to your liking, try being a guide at a museum. Whether it's natural history or modern art, you can again share knowledge with others and be in a setting you also enjoy.

❈ Become more active in your church. Most churches sponsor youth groups that can always use more helping hands and advice. There are usually study groups and orientation services for new members and other opportunities to keep you busy and in contact with other people.

These are only a few suggestions for worthwhile volunteer work. Check your local newspaper's weekly calendars or ask around to find other groups that need your help.

Learn To Live In The Present

Do you ever find yourself thinking: "Things were better for me last year (or two years ago or three or...)?" Or, "I'll still be alone when the holidays roll around and I'll feel badly all over again."

Clinging to an idea that your life was better in the past or worrying about how you *might* feel at some time in the future is counterproductive to feeling better about yourself now. It's important for you to learn to live in the here and now if you want to be comfortable with yourself.

As Dr. Richard Carlson, Ph.D., writes in his book *Don't Sweat The Small Stuff,* "Our peace of mind is determined by how much we are able to live in the present moment.

"Irrespective of what happened yesterday or last year and what may or may not happen tomorrow, the present moment is where you are – always! Practice keeping your attention on the here and now. Your efforts will pay great dividends."

How can you learn to live in the present moment? Look around you. Pay close attention to what is going on. That can mean taking a moment to watch the sun set in the evening or watching it rise in the morning. It might mean pausing along your walkway to watch a butterfly flitter around a colorful flowering bush. It can mean sitting on a park bench and watching children play on a swing set.

It means, basically, paying attention to whatever is going on around you. Because what is going on around you is *life* and it's happening each and every day. If you spend time thinking and stewing about the past or worrying and wondering about the future, you can miss the life that is going on around you right now, in the present moment. And once that particular present moment is gone, it's gone forever!

How can you live in the present moment? One good way to learn how is to study meditation. Mindfulness meditation focuses on the very moment of each breath you take. It is taught in many spiritual centers, new age centers and now even health clinics.

Mindfulness is even a key component of the Stress Reduction and Relaxation Program at the University of Massachusetts. Its director, Dr. Jon Kabat-Zinn, says mindfulness is the disciplined practice of moment-to-moment awareness. "All it involves is cultivating our ability to pay attention in the present moment," writes Kabat-Zinn in his book *Full Catastrophe Living*.

Kabat-Zinn teaches a simple mindfulness technique, a breathing exercise that you should practice every day:

1. Sit on the floor or on a chair that allows your feet to be flat on the floor.

2. Sit erect, keeping your head, neck and back in a straight line.

3. Bring your full attention to your breathing. Breathe from your belly – it expands with each in breath and recedes with each out breath.

4. Learn to simply *be* with each breath.

5. If your mind wanders off your breathing, note what distracted you, then gently bring your attention back to your breathing. No matter how often your mind wanders off or what caused it to do so, always bring its attention back to your breathing.

6. Practice this for at least 15 minutes each day. And be aware that what you are doing with this exercise is absolutely nothing except being with your breathing, in the moment.

With this exercise, writes Kabat-Zinn, "You are training your mind to be less reactive and more stable. You are making each moment count. You are taking each moment as it comes, not valuing any one above any other. In this way, you are cultivating your natural ability to concentrate your mind. It is a systematic way of teaching your body and mind to develop calmness within or beneath anxious feelings."

It also teaches you to keep yourself in the moment. Right now, you are alone and not being in the moment with your aloneness can cause you anxiety and grief. Learning to be with your aloneness – and yourself – can help you tremendously as you move through life.

How It All Works

Remember Marianne, the nurse from Los Angeles? Using many of the techniques described in this chapter, Marianne was able to make some big changes in her life. She no longer feels she is incomplete without a man and this has brought some very positive things into her life.

For one thing, her relationship with her sister Lisa is much improved. The two are no longer at odds over Marianne's irrational behaviors. Lisa and Marianne feel much more comfortable with each other and this comfort level shows in their interactions together.

"Now, when Marianne and I spend time together, we *really* spend time together," Lisa states. "We no longer spend all our time dealing with Marianne's latest crisis. It used to be that she talked and cried and I listened. Then I told her what I thought and she got mad. Then I got mad and we began shouting at each other, until we were into full-blown fights. We never really did anything together that we enjoyed and certainly nothing to make us feel closer to each other."

Marianne agrees.

"Lisa and I were always close as kids. My problems were driving a huge wedge between us. If I hadn't caught it in time, there may have been irreparable damage to our relationship. My sister – and all my family – is very important to me. I'm so glad that my therapy helped the two of us, too."

Marianne also points to how much she now enjoys being alone.

"I always used to dread getting up in the morning to a big empty house. I always thought I had to have someone in the bed next to me, someone peering at me over the top of the morning newspaper at the table," she says.

"But now, I truly enjoy getting up at the crack of dawn, taking a cup of steaming coffee onto my back porch and watching the sun come blazing up. It's become a routine and very spiritual experience for me, one that I look forward to each night when I go to bed. It's a special moment that I get to spend with myself each day and I really love it. I wouldn't give up my sunrises for anything!"

Well, almost. The other big change in Marianne's life is that she no longer finds herself attracted and attached to men who are toxic to her well-being. She is currently enjoying her life alone and has not yet found that special man. But Marianne is ready for – and looking forward to – having a special man to share her sunrises with.

"The best part about all this is that I know I can bring someone into my life who will be perfect for me!" she says enthusiastically. "I'm feeling so much better about myself, I know that I'm projecting that good feeling. I know people are picking up on it, too, because even my friends have noticed that something has changed. They can't quite put their finger on it, but they know.

"And men are noticing, too. Men who come up and talk to me when I'm out are different from the ones who used to be drawn to me. In fact, there are more men than ever introducing themselves to me and striking up conversations.

"It wasn't easy, making all these changes in my life. But the work was definitely worth the results. Now whenever I go out, I'm almost never dancing alone! And I love it."

How To Attract Someone Special Into Your Life

People can subconsciously keep themselves from having relationships for several reasons. One is that they fear negative and painful experiences just like ones they may have had in the past. It's possible for someone to get into a pattern of picking the same negative type of person over and over again. If this is what's happening to you, there are ways to break the cycle and attract the right person into your life.

Looking For Mr. Right – Finding Mr. Wrong

"I never meet the right kind of guys!"

"Men! They're all the same!"

"Why do I always end up dating the same man over and over?"

Good question! If you find yourself using words like "always" and "never," you're probably caught in a relationship pattern. And if you keep picking the wrong men over and over again, getting hurt each time the relationship ends badly, is it any wonder you're dancing alone now? You subconsciously ask yourself: Why go through all that pain and anguish again, when I know exactly what's going to happen?

So you've had bad relationships in the past. Everyone has. And we never forget them. While there may have been lots of positive and happy things in the same relationships, it seems all we can remember – in excruciating detail – are the bad times. We cling to them like life preservers and indeed we begin to think of these negative experiences as life preservers. By holding onto them, we convince ourselves to avoid getting into another relationship in order to keep ourselves from getting hurt again.

What we need to do is quite simple: Get over it!

Isn't your back getting tired from lugging all that old baggage around? Let's face it: It's safer to hang onto old "war stories" because they can be used as excuses to keep from taking a chance, from risking your heart on another relationship.

Have you ever made statements like these?

- ❦ It's not worth the trouble of going through another relationship. I was hurt too badly last time.

- ❦ I don't have the energy (time, money, nice clothes) to go out to the clubs (or anywhere) and try to meet someone right now.

- ❦ If I get into another relationship, it will just end up like all the others – with me getting hurt.

- ❦ I'm better off alone.

Poisonous Relationship Patterns

Are you stuck in a cycle of attracting the same type of man over and over again? Do you have any idea why you do this? Anne, a 39-year-old sales associate, attracted Mr. Wrong for many years – with serious consequences.

Anne had been married early in life to James, a dashing military officer. The two were madly in love and Anne finally had the things she thought she'd always wanted – a home, a child and an exciting life traveling the world. She and James lived a good life for many years, until one day, Anne's world came crashing in on her.

She discovered that James had been having an affair. This was the absolute last thing she'd ever expected to happen. Never in her wildest dreams did she think that the love of her life would do this to her. Anne was so crushed that she took their daughter Jennie and left immediately to go home to her mother's. She never went back. After a short time, Anne filed for divorce and vowed that no one would ever hurt her so badly again.

As the next few years passed, Anne dated a variety of men, but soon her friends began to notice that most of these men had something in common. When Anne hooked up with Joey and let him move in with her, her closest friend Nancy suddenly saw what all the men had in common.

"They could have all been related," she says. "They all had the same personality. They even looked the same. They walked and talked the same way, even dressed the same way. And what amazed me is that this was *not* the type of man Anne would normally have been interested in."

The very dark side of these men is that they loved to control women. Joey was no different. He made Anne's life so miserable that her friends begged her to kick him out. He belittled Anne and made her feel like she was nothing without him. For that reason, she couldn't possibly have let go of him.

Finally, life became unbearable. Anne's friends literally dragged her out of her own house and thus began a painful process of trying to get Joey out of her life. Anne finally accomplished it. But she was so beaten down by the experience that she decided to move to another state and start life all over again. Nancy, her best friend, moved with Anne.

"Moving or running away, as I called it, didn't do a thing for Anne's problem," recalls Nancy. "She went right back into the pattern of picking the same miserable type of guy again. This went on for another couple years until finally I started to get a clue why she was doing this. Now, I'm not a therapist, but if Anne had gone to one years before, she might have uncovered this and been able to stop her poisonous relationship pattern long ago."

During a long late-night talk, the subject of James came up. And Nancy was stunned to see Anne burst into tears, crying heaving sobs of pure anguish.

"You would have thought that she'd just found out yesterday that he was cheating on her," says Nancy. "And it had been years! It seemed she still felt as hurt that night as she did the day she found out James was cheating on her. As she babbled on and on about what he did to her, I suddenly realized something."

What Nancy realized is that all the men Anne chose

after her divorce were, in almost all respects, the polar opposite of James. It seemed that Anne was trying desperately to *not* ever have another man in her life who was even vaguely like James.

"What amazed me is that she really meant to not have someone like him. Even if that meant she got treated badly, she kept going out with these guys, apparently because they were so unlike James," Nancy says. "When I discussed this with her, she hotly denied it at first. But I could see the light of realization on her face, too. I think that after all these years, she was surprised to find a possible answer to why she kept getting herself into bad relationships. I think she even surprised herself."

Anne's quest for someone to love her and give her a good life like the one she had with James actually took her further away from her goal. Because she didn't want to be hurt again as badly as James had hurt her, she actually sabotaged herself with bad relationships. The pain she endured in her recent relationships somehow wasn't as deep as the pain she felt when James had cheated on her. She was able to handle her current pains, but still hadn't gotten over James.

Experts say Anne's situation isn't uncommon. We often try to avoid old pains and heartaches by doing whatever we can that is opposite of our situation that hurt us. Sometimes, that means selecting partners who are wrong for us. We don't consciously go out and say, "I'm going to meet someone who's bad for me."

But subconsciously, we may simply want to find a reason, an excuse to stay alone, even if that's not what we really want.

Could you be doing this? Let's go on a search for

some answers. Once you know why you go after the same Mr. Wrong, you'll know how to avoid him in the future.

Let's do some digging into your past:

1. List your last three to five relationships. List only relationships that lasted at least two months.

2. Describe each person physically. What does he look like? What kind of clothes does he wear? How does he walk and talk and use his body language? Is there some particular quirk or habit he has, like always winking at you or holding your hand a certain way?

3. Describe each person's personality. Is he boisterous or quiet? The life of the party or a wallflower? Does he love sports or the opera? Is he open about himself or secretive? Be as specific as you can.

4. List everything you liked about each person. (But don't be surprised if you have trouble coming up with many things. Often, in retrospect, we find that there wasn't much we liked about someone.)

5. List everything you didn't like about each person – and yes, there were plenty of things you didn't like. Maybe he snored or was always late or spent too much time with his friends watching sports on television. Write it all down.

6. Now make a new list by pulling out all the things that each of these different people appear to have in common. Whether it's looks, personality or things you liked and disliked, pull together everything that shows up commonly amongst the men.

7. Look at the result. Do you see the description of a person who could be any of the people you've listed? You may have constructed your generic "Mr. Wrong." Look at him carefully. Because now you have to ask yourself: Will I meet him again? The answer is most likely: YES! And now the question will be: Can I avoid becoming involved with someone who's wrong for me? Read on.

8. What attracted you to each of these men in the first place? What drew you to first notice them? Were there signals in the beginning that told you this guy was wrong, too? And did you ignore those signals? Why?

    This item calls for lots of introspection. You may see where you actually were warned that this was Mr. Wrong all over again, but for some reason, you chose to ignore the warning signs.

9. Try to recall how you were feeling at the time. Were you feeling extremely lonely? Exceptionally needy?

You may be surprised to find that you really did know the guy was wrong for you. Perhaps now, if you see those signs again, you can turn on your heel and march confidently in the opposite direction, knowing that you've saved yourself a lot of anguish and left yourself open for the *real* Mr. Right.

Create Your Mr. Right

Now that you've discovered who Mr. Wrong is, do a similar exercise to find out who your Mr. Right is. By putting down on paper what it is you're looking for, you can solidify an image in your mind that can help you attract just that type of person.

1. Describe the physical appearance of the person you seek. Physical appearance should not be the only factor about someone you seek, of course. But there must be some idea in your mind of what the person might look like.

2. Describe the personality of the person you seek. Be as specific as you can. Do you want someone who is the life of the party or does the strong, silent type affect you more?

3. Now list all the qualities you seek in a relationship. These will be items beyond appearance and personality. For example: "I want someone who wouldn't mind missing a football game on TV to take his children to the movies." Or, "I want someone who can talk with me – and listen – instead of shouting and getting angry if we have a misunderstanding or disagreement."

4. Using this description of your Mr. Right, you can work with positive affirmations to help bring him into your life. As you learned about writing positive affirmations for self-esteem boosting, you can write affirmations about the relationship you seek, based on the information you've listed in this exercise.

Using the examples above, here are two affirmations:

✔ I deserve a man who respects me enough to talk with me and listen rather than fight with me if we have a misunderstanding or disagreement.

✔ Caring, thoughtful men are attracted to me and come into my life easily.

Work with your affirmations daily to help draw Mr. Right into your life.

He's Not Wrong, But Is He Mr. Compatible?

Now that you know how to spot what's wrong with a man, here's a way to look for what's right! According to Los Angeles-based relationship psychologist Yvonne Thomas, Ph.D., in *Seventeen* magazine, there are five essential elements of compatibility. Check out your next prospect to see if he's compatible with you in these ways:

1. Intellect. This is about your intelligence in relation to each other and what types of things challenge each of you.

If one of you has a college degree and the other one doesn't, this does not mean you aren't compatible. As long as you are able to relate to each other and enjoy many common interests, this will not be a negative factor in your relationship.

But if there are differences and one of you puts the other down, it's time to walk away.

2. Emotional. This involves your maturity levels, identities and relationships.

Have you ever been with a man who you felt acted like a spoiled child or a wild teenager? No wonder you weren't compatible if you were trying to have a mature, adult relationship! Make sure the man you're interested in is at least as old as you are mentally and emotionally.

3. Philosophical. This involves your life beliefs

(such as religion) and your personal views of the world around you.

Can an atheist and a believer find happiness together? Can an animal-lover have a great relationship with someone who doesn't like animals? Maybe. But the odds are greatly against them. You're better off picking someone with beliefs and views similar to your own.

4. *Physical*. This is about how comfortable you are with your appearance and your sexuality.

Two people can be sexually incompatible – for example, his sexual appetite is stronger than hers, he enjoys doing things during sex that she doesn't. During the early stages of a relationship, when everything about it is highly charged, you may not notice such differences too much. But later on, they can become quite apparent and cause great conflict in a relationship. It pays to be alert to such differences early in the relationship.

5. *Lifestyle*. This can include everything from hobbies to friends to habits and more.

He's up at the crack of dawn, but you've been a rather nocturnal creature all your life. He likes sports bars, you like art galleries. He hates the sun, you love the beach. Can you make it together? Maybe. But again, these are all things in your different lifestyles that can clash and cause conflict. Pay close attention to things such as this, too, and how they affect you in the early stages of a relationship.

If you and your prospective guy click on a couple of the items above, you're on the right road. But it's important to emphasize that the above list is just a guideline. When it comes to two people, to their hearts and emotions, nothing is written in stone. But if you want to up your chances of pairing with someone you can have and hold, the odds are more with you if you're at least compatible from the start.

Where To Find Men

If it's been a while since you've had someone in your life, you may have become stuck in your thinking that the only place to meet someone is at singles' bars. Wrong! In fact, you're likely to find a compatible Mr. Right almost anywhere you go to pursue your interests and hobbies.

Perhaps you like the singles' bar scene and that's okay too, if it fits your tastes. But if not, you may want to try places where groups of people gather for business or social settings. Consider these different places to meet new men:

Sports clubs. Finding a group for a sports activity you enjoy will put you in touch with men who share your interests. Check your town's Department of Recreation for adults sports schedules and to find a team to join if you like volleyball, softball or bowling. Find a roller skating club or start going regularly to a roller rink which will also have events and meets. If biking and running appeal to you, find a local group that has regular outings.

Dance lessons. You'll likely find plenty of men taking dance lessons for the same reasons you are – to feel good, to be confident and to meet new people. Ballroom dancing is always in style and the best thing about it is it requires partners! Most dance studios hold regular mixers so clients can practice their dance lessons on a regular basis. This way, you'll keep in constant touch with the men you meet in class and the two of you can try out your new moves on the dance floor together! Sounds like fun.

Chamber of Commerce meetings. This is a terrific place to meet new men and also pick up some valuable contacts to further your career goals and add to your self-esteem in the process. Members of your town's Chamber can run the gamut from small businessmen to the Chairman of the Board of a large corporation. The atmosphere at meetings and social gatherings is part business and part pleasure and they generally occur during daytime hours, so you'll find a level of comfort you might not find if you hit the nighttime bar scene right away.

Volunteer your time. Your community will provide plenty of opportunities to perform volunteer work to help others. Not only will you meet caring, giving people when working for charity organizations, but you'll add to your self-esteem and feel good about yourself for helping others. You can volunteer to work at hospitals, children's organizations, libraries, humane societies and charities such as the Red Cross.

Dog training classes. How many times have you heard or read about a couple who met while walking their dogs? Meet other true dog fanciers at obedience school where you can admire each other's best friends and becomes friends (and maybe lovers) yourselves! Pets are a great ice-breaker and an immediate common interest that's easy for both of you to talk about. Find the most popular dog obedience school in your area and sign up your dog.

Women's gatherings and groups. Yes, you can meet men at women's groups, too. How? By first meeting new women friends who might have brothers, cousins, co-workers and male friends that they would be glad to introduce to you! Try exercise classes, women's business groups, self-defense courses or the YWCA. Besides, it never hurts to expand your circle of acquaintances and in this way add a little something more to your life.

A singles' resort. Treat yourself to a weekend trip and enjoy a touch of exotica at the same time. Many resorts cater to single people, but do so in a way that is easy-going. Prearranged activities make it easy to meet new men in a group setting, but you can also quietly sneak away later on your own if you happen to meet someone who clicks with you.

If you get involved in activities you enjoy, you will naturally put yourself into situations where you'll meet new people, including new men. So get out there and savor life and you'll do fine!

The New You

It's been a while since you've dated. In fact, it's been a while since you've had a confident attitude that will attract a man! Sure, it's a little scary. And now that you know where to look for Mr. Right, you're standing in front of your closet, looking at your clothes and wondering if you shouldn't just put on your jammies and jump right into bed instead!

If going out actively looking again makes you wonder what to wear, how to act and what to say once you do start meeting men, here are some tips gathered from a group of women who have no problem attracting men no matter where they go!

What To Wear

✔ Examine your style of dress and consider changing it. If you can't change your style of dress where you work, then go home and change before you go out. If you're comfortable with the idea, try some tighter, more revealing clothing for evening wear. If that's not your thing, find sexy, drapey clothing that swirls and flows along your body's lines. Either way, it's a lush look that's sexy and alluring. And don't forget jewelry! It doesn't have to be expensive. Worn properly to accent your features, jewelry will make you stand out in a crowd.

✔ Want to get really wild? Try some animal print clothing, such as tiger, leopard or zebra patterned pants and tops. There's something absolutely feral about the look and it can bring out the animal in a man! But be honest with yourself when you're trying these types of clothes on for the first time – do you look fabulous or completely silly? Some women can wear animal print clothes and, unfortunately, some can't. If you can't, find another sexy look for yourself (such as lace or suede or silk).

✔ Another sexy look is to show your back. While lots of women focus on wearing low-cut dresses and blouses to show off cleavage, they often overlook how alluring a bare back can be. Look for dresses that are cut to the waist in the back. When you find one, learn to roll your shoulders elegantly.

✔ Look at your makeup. Is it in need of an overhaul? Go to a department store's makeup department for a makeover. Pay attention to how the professionals apply the makeup during the makeover. If you learn professional techniques for applying makeup, you'll always look picture-perfect. And there's nothing sexier than a woman who can wear makeup without looking made-up!

Then go to your drugstore and copy that expensive look. Buy new eye shadows, liners, lipstick, pencils, blushes and mascara. Flaunt all the latest makeup styles and new colors.

✔ If your hair is long, think about keeping it that way. Men love long hair, it's as simple as that. Surveys say men find lush and long hair sexy.

Show your sexiness and individuality with your long hair by placing a fresh flower in it whenever you go out. In the Pacific islands, women wear flowers in their hair as a signal that they're available.

✔ If you prefer short hair, go for a bold and sassy cut that says this is exactly who and what you are! Be daring and trendy.

✔ Every now and then, it's fun to cover your hair with a sexy hat. If you're the type of woman who can wear a hat, do so! Men love hats. Try a sexy, head-hugging cloche or a mysterious fedora. You can make wearing a hat part of your identity.

✔ Never thought you could wear red before? Do it now! Red clothing is red-hot for going out at night and attracting men. Go for broke with a sleek red dress with a slit up the side. If you're more on the subtle side, try a lacy red slip. When you sit down, cross your legs and let your skirt ride up a bit to reveal just a hint of the red slip – oo-la-la!

✔ Perhaps your style is more lacy and romantic, a

look men also love. Try long, flowered dresses with a peek-a-boo neckline. Wear your hair soft and curly, cascading over your shoulders and framing your face. Or sweep it up into an elegant bun with sexy, curly tendrils hanging down. This softer romantic look can be worn for everyday as well and will do just as much as the fiery nighttime look as far as attracting a man's attention.

✔ Wear fragrance. It can take some time, but shop around until you find a fragrance that is YOU. As you know, different women's body chemistry reacts differently to the same fragrance. This is why you can take a popular fragrance and find that on you it smells different than on your friends. When you find a scent that is uniquely you, it becomes your signature, something a man will remember about you. And whenever he smells the fragrance, his mind will immediately go to you!

Spray the fragrance lightly on your pulse points before you get dressed. Be sure to take a purse-size bottle of the fragrance with you so you can freshen up throughout the day or evening. Here's a special tip: Before you get dressed, spray the fragrance into the air in front of you, then quickly walk into the mist. This distributes the fragrance evenly over your entire body and you don't have any fragrance "hot spots" where the scent is too strong!

What To Do And How To Act

You want to act sexy without being in-his-face or overbearing. You also don't want to put on a fake sexy come-on. Here are some subtle, yet sexy tricks to try:

✔ Go ahead and make the first move. Men get tired of having to speak to women first. Catch his eye and smile, then hold his gaze for a few seconds. Perhaps you can quickly scan him up and down, but do it while you're smiling and he'll surely feel flattered. Then you can approach him – just say hello and start a conversation. You're sure to keep his attention once you show him your intelligence and dazzle him with your sparkling personality!

✔ After you've got his attention (whether you talked to him first or he talked to you), find a subtle way to touch him. Brush his arm gently when you laugh at something or brush away a piece of imaginary lint from his lapel. By making even a minimal and brief physical contact, you tell him that you're interested. If you can, gently brush the top of his hand. This little move can send shivers down his spine!

✔ Act confident and relaxed. Hold your head up high (stretch that beautiful neck!) and pull your chin down toward your chest slightly. Keep your shoulders back. Rest your hands lightly on the table or in your lap and make sure you aren't "white-knuckling" out of nervousness. The more confident and relaxed you are, the more comfortable he'll be around you. In fact, a sexy way to show how confident and relaxed you are is to gently kick your shoes off while you sit and talk with him. You'll really grab his attention with your sexy, pedicured feet, too!

✔ Show your confidence in yourself on the dance floor. Be sure to swing your hips with the music and move your body to the beat. The sexier you dance, the better! Practice your moves at home in front of a mirror if you're not used to doing sexy dances.

✒ Be yourself. You're a real and down-to-earth person, not a Barbie doll. And in a world full of dolls, you can stand head and shoulders above the crowd by being real. Show that you appreciate yourself and he will know that you're worthy of his appreciation.

✒ When you leave, grasp his hand warmly and firmly and hold on while you say your goodbye. You could also hold his hand and place your other hand gently on his shoulder while you tell him what a wonderful time you had dancing and chatting with him. If you're really feeling like you want to impress him, give him a goodbye kiss on the cheek.

✒ Don't have a stranger take you home. It's best that strangers not know where you live until you've had time to get to know one another. You simply don't have any idea who you're dealing with at first. Avoid putting yourself into shaky or even dangerous positions by driving yourself home or calling a taxi.

What To Say

✒ It's difficult to talk if you have to shout above loud music or a boisterous crowd of people, so if you want the attention of the man you've just met, invite him to join you at a quiet table or in another room. This way you can get to know each other better without yelling in each other's ears.

✒ Contribute to the conversation. Men don't like having to do all the talking when they first meet a woman. Take that pressure off him and go 50-50 with the talking. Talk about yourself, but make sure you talk about him, too. Ask him questions about himself and spend time listening to what he's saying, which shows you're truly interested. Compliment him on his clothes, hair, shoes or whatever you like about him.

✔ Be sure you're wearing your best sense of humor. A woman who is clever, witty and entertaining is highly desirable to men, who can't pull themselves away from her! Think of how much fun you have chatting with a sharp, witty man.

✔ Don't tell him everything about yourself on the first date. Men love women who keep an air of mystery about themselves. Give out information a little bit at a time and this way he'll want to know more. Then you'll have things to talk about on later dates if all goes well.

✔ Avoid talking about depressing subjects. Work problems, financial woes and other downers are taboo when meeting a new man! And especially don't talk about ex-lovers/husbands/boyfriends, particularly if all you have to talk about is bad experiences with them. War stories don't belong in conversations between two people who've just met. If a man talked badly about his ex-girlfriend, you'd think twice about continuing your conversation with him, right?

✔ If the subject of exes does come up, however, speak about your ex with civility. A new man will notice this and respect it. But don't dwell on the subject. Try to get on to more important topics between the two of you.

✔ Talk about yourself in a positive light. Sure, you've just started going out again after being alone (and depressed) for a while, but don't tell him that! And don't list all your shortcomings. Instead of seeing the good things about you, he may indeed begin to focus on what you've told him you think is wrong with yourself. How would you feel if a new man told you all the bad things about himself? You'd probably run in the opposite direction!

✔ Talk about positive things. Your interests, hobbies, your children, friends and other wonderful, fun things about yourself will make a new man want to see you again. Let your personality shine through!

✔ Be honest about your intentions. If a man tells you he's looking for a wife and you're simply not ready to think about that level of commitment, say so. Be up front about where you stand, so you can prevent hurt feelings later on. Make sure no one misunderstands the other person's situation and feelings.

✔ Keep your conversation in the present and keep them pleasant. Leave out heavy topics such as past traumas and possible futures. You don't want to scare off a hot prospect by looking too far down the road. Would you be comfortable if a man you barely knew talked that way to you?

✔ Don't start – or let yourself be drawn into – sexual conversations with a stranger that make you and/or him feel uncomfortable. If he starts it, you don't have to pick up on it – it likely means that sex is a high priority for him. If you start it, you may push away a very well-intentioned man who is looking for a real human connection first, not a physical one.

Something To Remember

Past bad experiences may have been the key factor in keeping you without a dance partner. Now that you're out looking again and know how to avoid picking Mr. Wrong, you must remember to resist the urge to compare potential new loves to your former loves who hurt you. If you keep comparing them and carrying around your old baggage, you're not truly opening yourself to finding love and ending your loneliness. You are living in the past.

Remember, the idea is to get yourself to move forward. Even if your heart has been broken in the past and you're now dancing alone, you must remember that everyone is an individual.

Allow new men you meet to be themselves and don't compare them to your former loves who hurt you. If you accept each person for who he is, you may find that there are plenty of wonderful, caring men out there who can fill your dance card.

You don't have to be lonely any more! Just accept each person you meet for who he is.

How To Keep Someone In Your Life

It's called "relationship maintenance." It's what you should do in order to keep everything healthy and happy between the two of you. Sure, your lives are hectic. But you have to invest time in maintaining the relationship you worked so hard to get in the first place. You want to have the relationship that your friends point to with jealousy. You want to be the storybook couple you've always dreamed you'd be. That won't happen if you don't make a conscious effort to keep the relationship healthy.

How can you do that? Don't worry if you can't immediately answer the question. Even the most perfect relationships can use a tune-up now and then and some advice and tips on how to keep it going.

Here are some suggestions on how to keep your relationship in perfect health, according to Barry Spilchuk, author of *A Cup of Chicken Soup for the Soul* and the new interactive program, *Let's Talk About Relationships*.

1. *Don't let the little things bug you.* It's all a matter of perspective. In the course of a lifetime, what does it matter if he sometimes brings the car home with a nearly empty gas tank? Some things in life are important and other things aren't. Deciding which is which can be the difference between harmony and discord in your relationship.

2. *Let go of the need to always be right.* Well, you say, somebody has to be right and somebody has to be wrong, right? No. In fact, Spilchuk asks, "Do you want to be right or do you want to be happy?"

3. *Be in love, but be independent.* Have you ever known someone who couldn't let their partner go to the corner market alone? Or talk to someone on the telephone without their partner interrupting or vying for their attention? Just because you're part of a couple doesn't mean you lose your own identity. It's important for both of you to be independent and to have alone time even if you're together. (Yes, you can be alone together.)

Says Spilchuk: "It scares me when one person relies on the other even to keep them breathing."

4. *Discuss your feelings as they come up.* Nothing is worse than allowing bad feelings to simmer and stew. They keep you in a foul mood and keep your partner unaware that anything is wrong until you suddenly spring it on him. Better to get it over with than to drag it out for long periods of time.

5. *Practice self-love.* Keep up with all the exercises and tips you learned about raising your self-esteem, not only because you want to feel better, but because lack of self-love will have you concentrating on your faults. And more.

"If you don't love yourself, you're going to find all the flaws in yourself and in your partner," cautions Spilchuk.

6. *Be the first to say, "I'm sorry" and the first to forgive.* Again, why draw things out over long periods of time? Get the bad feelings over with. And show you're a good sport by trying to be first to forgive and forget.

"It's good when couples race to do that!" Spilchuk adds.

7. *Never withhold love.* If you're in a situation where you're having some problems or disagreements, remember that you don't simply stop loving your partner. So why would you withhold love? Doing so can cause bad feelings that may take too long to repair, if they can be repaired.

8. *Laugh a lot.* It's true that if you laugh, the world laughs with you. That's especially true in a relationship. Laughing a lot – together – is like super-glue! It bonds you more firmly with each use. So laugh and have fun!

Making Time To Talk

When you say something to a person who's important to you, don't you want them to listen to you? To hear what you're saying? And listening to him is an extremely important part of keeping your relationship healthy. With today's busy world and both of you leading hectic lives, it seems you don't have enough hours in the day to accomplish everything you have to do, let alone sit down and spend time talking with someone.

But experts keep reminding us that the key to having and keeping a fantastic relationship is communication. So if you don't have time to talk, make the time!

Here are some suggestions for finding more time in your busy day:

1. *Do chores together – and use that time to talk.* If you both enjoy gardening, get those flowers put in or pull those weeds out together. You get your yard work done in half the time, but you also get to cooperate on a project together and that encourages you to talk as you work.

2. *Drive to work together.* If it's possible and you can make your two schedules fit, drive to and from work together each day. Even if it's a few minutes out of the way for one of you, you can pool your travel expenses and save some money on gas and parking fees. Plus, the travel time – and possibly sitting in heavy traffic time – can be spent talking together. It's found time.

3. *Spruce up your house (or his) together.* Once again, four hands are more efficient than two and you'll get that furniture refinished or that kitchen painted in half the time. You'll also spend quality time together.

4. *Exercise together.* If you go to the gym together, for example, try doing your warm-ups on side-by-side stationary bikes, treadmills or stair-stepper machines. You can chat together a bit, even if you're working out and running out of breath. If you prefer outdoor workouts, you can run, bike or swim together.

5. *Go out for dinner.* You don't have to go anywhere fancy or expensive. Just somewhere that serves good food you enjoy and gives you a quiet setting where you can talk together while someone else does the cooking (and cleaning up afterward).

Little Things Mean A Lot

Sometimes it's the little things in life that keep people together. Doing little things for each other shows a deep caring, something that goes beyond the superficial and can last for, well, forever!

Here are some suggestions from experts on little things you can do that can mean a lot in a relationship:

✤ Some morning, slip a little note into your partner's briefcase, lunchbox or something he takes to work with him. In the note, say something simple, such as, "I can't wait to see you after work this evening," or "Just to let you know I'm thinking of you." Finding the note once he gets to work will certainly brighten his day. It will give him a pleasant little surprise and a reassurance that you are thinking of him and you don't even have to say "I love you."

✤ Leave little "IOUs" for him to find, such as "IOU one hug this evening," or "IOU a special dinner tonight." This not only gives him something to look forward to, but it makes him feel good that you're making "little promises" to him, showing you care and are committed to him.

✤ Make a list of things your partner likes, such as a foot massage or a movie date. Then each day, do one of the things on your list for your partner. He'll be receiving that special attention he likes each day, a constant reminder that you love him.

✤ Give a little gift to your partner for no particular reason. Aside from birthdays, Valentine's Day, Christmas or anniversaries, a surprise gift is a sure way to say "I love you."

Make the gift something special. If your partner has a hobby, tie the gift into that. For example, if he likes to put together jigsaw puzzles, getting him a new puzzle as a surprise really shows you're thinking about him and what he enjoys. Flowers and candy are timeless, romantic and always appreciated and they're traditional for sending the message "I love you." And there's nothing wrong with you sending flowers or candy to a man if he appreciates them.

❧ Fix your loved one a special gourmet meal at home. Make sure you're alone for the evening, use the best dishes and set a beautiful table with flowers and candles. Get a bottle of your favorite wine or champagne and make sure your mate's favorite music is playing in the background.

❧ Write a poem for your loved one – it's a very personal thing and it says so much more than the spoken word. It's also something that can be saved and treasured, re-read over and over. It's not gone in an instant like spoken words, and when you write a poem you take time to choose the best words you can to say what you want your loved one to know.

❧ Arrange to take a special trip together. Plan a romantic getaway that sends the two of you off on your own, away from work and all your worries. Choose a destination that both of you have wanted to visit or somewhere you've been before that has wonderful memories for you. Surprising your mate with a special trip really says "I love you."

❧ You can show you care by trying to look your best. Wear clothes that your mate likes to see you wear. Be sure to use that special perfume or cologne that your mate really likes and wear your hair in his favorite styles. If you have jewelry he has given you, make sure you wear it, especially if you are going out somewhere. It shows your appreciation for the gift and your feelings for the giver.

✤ Be very creative and come up with more things you can do to make your partner feel special. There are so many ways to say "I love you" without actually saying the words. And sometimes doing it in this way speaks louder than the words.

Just remember that whatever you do shouldn't be perceived as something that was coming to your partner anyway. Rather, it should be seen as something you've really taken the time out to think about, something that says "I love you" without words.

Saving A Troubled Relationship

Often, the spark goes out of a relationship if you don't pay attention to it. Suppose you do run into a few rough spots with your relationship? First, you have to ask yourself if this relationship is something you want to save. It might not be.

But if it is, you can save the relationship if you work on it. You may need to rejuvenate and reinvent a courtship with your partner so you regain the feelings you had when you first got together.

First, here are some signs that a relationship might be on shaky ground:

✤ Changes in grooming. If your partner is getting sloppy, he may no longer care about looking good for you. On the other hand, if he's paying more attention to his grooming than he has in a long time, could there be someone else he has an eye on?

You might even try recreating the night you first met to feel that first spark of excitement again.

✤ Make a "care" list of the top ten things your partner likes, such as a relaxing massage or a special dinner. Do all the things on the list over a week's time. Have your partner put together a care list for you. By doing this, you will be showering attention on each other and spending quality time together.

✤ Don't try to read your partner's mind or make assumptions about his feelings. Ask specific questions and let your partner speak for himself. If you let your own imagination run wild with assumptions and guesswork, you'll never communicate constructively.

✤ Talk about everything that's bothering you. Don't hold anything back, but be careful not to do it all at once. You don't want a deluge of talk. But opening up in this way will often bring a new closeness and warmth to your relationship.

✤ Don't get into a stand-off about who is going to change first in the relationship – you'll get nowhere. Take the initiative to start making positive changes in your own behavior and don't demand that your partner change. Your positive moves will inspire your partner to then take the same steps.

You're ready! You've come a long way and learned a lot. It's time to get out there and bring a dance partner into your life. Remember, when you're part of a couple, you're still two individual people. Each one of you is equally important, so don't ignore yourself even when you have a dance partner. If you always think of yourself as an important person, you won't have to dance alone anymore.

❋ Overeating. This can be a sign that your partner isn't feeling very good about himself, is depressed or no longer cares about his own appearance.

❋ Former sweetheart fantasies. If he starts to compare you to an old girlfriend, he may feel he's not getting what he wants out of the relationship.

❋ Overspending. This can be a way to fulfill a perceived need. He may feel his needs aren't being met in the relationship.

❋ Parent/family avoidance. If he's not feeling good about the relationship, he sure doesn't want to be around your family, who might sense that he's not happy.

❋ Shared experience withdrawal. If the two of you have always gone to the movies together on Tuesday nights, and he starts to find reasons to not go.

❋ Complaining to friends. If he's willing to tell friends he's not happy, then believe that he's not happy.

Is the relationship on the rocks? Here's what you might do:

❋ Put your relationship first, above everything else. If you want or need time alone together, tell your friends, relatives and children that you need time alone. Make arrangements for child care if you have to, so you can go off alone together for the evening.

❋ In addition to making special events out of birthdays and anniversaries, create your own special days and times. Do things your partner loves to do, for no particular reason other than for the relationship. Serve his favorite dinner, including his extra-favorite dessert.